A CIRCLE OF STONES

Teachings for Teens on Anishinaabe Culture

By R.J. Hejna

Bookman Publishing
Martinsville, Indiana
www.BookmanMarketing.com

© Copyright 2003, Rob Hejna

All Rights Reserved.

No part of this book may be reproduced, stored in
a retrieval system, or transmitted by any means,
electronic, mechanical, photocopying, recording,
or otherwise, without written permission
from the author.

ISBN: 1-932301-85-2

Illustration on Right Page:
Ojibway Man, Early 1900's
Courtesy Minnesota Historical Society

DEDICATION

A CIRCLE OF STONES is dedicated to Suzanne Downing, of Mt. Pleasant, Michigan; and all the countless other Anishinaabe infants and youth taken from their families by Social Service agencies, and placed in non-Native foster homes; thereby losing the opportunity to be raised in alignment with traditional values, or awareness of their heritage, language, and culture.

FOREWORD

In the spring of 1987, my life was changing in many ways. I was completing my third year of study on the Sweet Medicine SunDance Path, a set of guidelines for developing one's self toward inner balance and stability, and working as a School Social Worker in southeastern Michigan. Through my study, I gained a profound respect for the beauty and integrity of Native American philosophy. Through my connection with the schools, I became a volunteer with a government funded program of cultural renewal activities for Native American families. I wrote articles for their newsletter, helped recruit new members, lead discussion sessions, and supervised activities with the children. I began to notice how little the families knew about their heritage, and wondered why. As I started to look through textbooks used to teach Michigan History, I found only brief descriptions of the Michigan tribes. I also began to notice some racist attitudes in the schools toward Native American students. I inquired of parents of special education students whether they had Native ancestry, and found that it was true for over one third. In comparison, less than one twelfth of the total population of the district were identified as having Native ancestry, according to surveys done each year. Although this could not directly predict racism, it was significant. Only later, did I realize that the cumulative effect of two hundred years of racist government policy toward Native people has so deeply damaged their self esteem, that many families have taken frustration out on their members, through generations, creating children who feel hopeless and angry. I began to hear from Native students that they were being teased about their appearance, either called "nigger" or "taco". Many told me they wished they could learn more from experience, rather than through "bookwork". I found, in discussions with teachers, that most knew very little about Native values, traditions, or philosophy. Gradually, I started to understand why so many Native or part-Native children were being certified for special education services.

During the summer of 1987, I participated in a Native American style SunDance, sponsored by the Deer Tribe Metis Medicine Society in southwestern

United States. It was a powerful experience to fast and dance in a continuous state of prayer for a number of days. One of the answers to my prayers was a strong message that I should write a book for children about the values, traditions, and philosophy of the Great Lakes tribes. The goal would be to clear up misunderstandings and ignorance causing prejudice toward Native people. It would be to facilitate an increase in acceptance of Native heritage as being complex, dynamic, sophisticated, intelligent, and quite civilized. It would be to show that Native people are just as "human" in every way as any other people in the world—but have their own values and traditions, which are equally valid and worthy of respect as those of any other culture.

My first reaction to this message was to wonder how I could write such a book as a non-Native. Most of my experience had been with the Sweet Medicine Sundance Path, which blends various Native perspectives, but has its foundation in south-western and plains tribal orientation. I did not wish to intrude on Michigan Native life, or make a "study" of their culture. I decided to learn patience, look for opportunities, and wait for the project to evolve. I discovered wonderful books on Ojibway culture by talented Ojibway authors Basil Johnston, and Eddie Benton-Benai. I found numerous anthropological studies, and a thorough and scholarly book funded by the Michigan Indian Press, called <u>People of The Three Fires</u>. I attended a conference for Native educators, and Earth Renewal ceremonial weekends with Adam Fortunate Eagle Nordwall, Ojibway elder, author, spiritual leader, and artist from Minnesota. I visited the Family Life Education program at Lac Du Flambeau Ojibway Reservation, Wisconsin, which teaches traditional values, and heritage. I started to study Ojibway language with Hap McCue, Ojibway elder from Ontario, and met with people studying herbal healing with Keewadinoquay, Ojibway elder from Garden Island. I went to Pow-Wow's regularly, and let the feeling of "good-heartedness" flow into me from the songs, drum, and dance.

Slowly, a book has emerged. It has taken a few different formats, and been reviewed by members of the Ojibway Sage Council for Cultural Renewal, as well as by Fortunate Eagle, HapMcCue, Basil Johnston, and Eddie Benton-Benai. I have given it the title, <u>A CIRCLE OF STONES,</u> in honor of the Circle of Life, and all Councils, in which people from different views come together to find ways to coexist in as harmonious a way as possible. While I am aware that the traditional Native way to teach is through story form, my concern for providing a "credible" means for public educators to decrease prejudice leads me to use some straight sharing of information. It is one of those ironic differences in culture, that the dominant society in America puts more credence in factual information, while native culture regards strait fact as dry and potentially presumptuous. I have aimed the book toward middle and high school non-Native audiences. If A CIRCLE OF STONES turns out to be helpful to even one Anishinaabe teen, who discovers here a doorway to their own heritage, and decides to ask their edlers for more guidance—then I would feel very gratified indeed.

The chapters are labeled "stones" to symbolize the way elders in traditional times taught the children about the Circle of Life by placing a circle of stones on the ground. Each stone then was a door which opened a world of knowledge. The SAGE Council informed me that just four stones were more likely to have been used. I needed to divide the material into shorter sections, so I went with eight stones. I hope I do not offend anyone with this apparrent break from tradition.

An explanation is needed regarding the use of different spellings of Native words in the text. First, the grammatical nuances of Native language are quite complex, and reflect the complexity of the culture. "Anishinaabe" is singular. "Anishinaabeg" is plural. "Anishinaubek" denotes an animate representative aspect of the culture. Second, there are differing preferred ways of expressing, pronouncing, and spelling Native terms in different areas, bands, communities, even families. Anishinaabe is "Anishinaubae", and Anishinaubek spelled "Anishinaubaek" in some areas like Northern Ontario. But, as Basil Johnston pointed out to me, it is all One People, One Language. Hence I have chosen to sometimes use a term or spelling from Hap McCue, Eddie Benton-Benai, Basil Johnston, or from the Lac Du Flambeau program. They are merely intended to be examples of the Native language, provided to allow non-Native children to see that there really is a whole language, and not only words like "how".

I must acknowledge that the more I learn, the more I realize my knowledge is limited. I do not in any way presume to be an authority on Michigan Native culture. I only wish to present some information which may help to diminish fear and prejudice.

Finally, I pledge to contribute half of my share of any earnings from the sale of this book, to the Anishinaabe SAGE Council of elders and teachers who support, sponsor, and organize programs to educate Anishinaabe young people in the ways and knowledge of traditional culture.

Robert J. Hejna
Tibik Gibwa-nassi
Nighthawk

ACKNOWLEDGEMENTS

The Anishinaabe word most commonly used for "thank you" is "miigwetch" (mee-gwech). I have been told its true meaning is: I hold with honor that which you have given to me. I say miigwetch now to the many people who gave their energy and time, their wisdom and guidance to help make this book possible.

Miigwetch to the Parent Committee of the Airport Schools Title IV Indian Heritage program for loaning many valuable sources of information—many of which are listed in the bibliography.

Miigwetch to Dr. Adam Fortunate Eagle Nordwall, Ojibway elder, artist, author, spiritual leader, and pipemaker, for the talks and visits; and the experience of Anishinaabe ceremony. Thank you also for encouragement regarding the book.

Miigwetch to Basil Johnston O. Ont., LLD., BA., Ojibway elder, author, and ceremonialist for providing a careful and detailed critique of the book's contents.

Miigwetch to Dr. Eddie Benton-Benai, Ojibway elder, author, spiritual teacher, healer, and ceremonialist for reviewing the book and offering valuable consultation on format and style.

Miigwetch to members of the SAGE Council of Anishinaabe Elders, Ceremonialists, and Cultural Renewal Educators for reviewing the book, and meeting with me for guidance. Thank you to Bucko Teeple, Andrew LeBlanc, Donnie Dowd, and Beaver.

Miigwetch to Hap McCue, Ojibway elder, ceremonialist, and Lecturer in Ojibway language at University of Michigan for reviewing the book and meeting for many hours to discuss ways the culture is held in the language.

Miigwetch to Alton Sonny Smart, Ojibway teacher, ceremonialist, social worker, and founder of the Family Life Education program for cultural renewal at Lac Du Flambeau, Wisconsin for sharing information on traditional values. Thank you also to Tinker and others from the program for the hospitality on my visit there.

Miigwetch to Marsha Traxler, nurse, mshkiki healer, and student of

Keewadinoquay, for valuable information on her experience of Anishinaabe culture, and consultation regarding the focus and style of the book.

Miigwetch to my dear friend, Edwin Ian Simpson, artist and ceremonialist now dwelling in the Land of Souls, for design of the book's cover. Thanks to Dr. Steve Chensue and Michael Thompson for providing illustrations. M.T. created the shield designs for chapter title pages.

Miigwetch to the staffs of the Minnesota, Wisconsin, Grand Rapids, and Bentley Historical Societies and Libraries, and the National Anthropological Archives for access to photograph archives.

Miigwetch to Janet Seddon, overseer and trustee for the Susan Eleanor Boulet Trust. It is truly an honor to have included three of Susan's prints in a part of the book which needed the touch of spirit.

Kitchi Miigwetch to those unidentified Anishinaabe who appear in historical photographs in this book. I acknowledge that these photographs may have been stolen by whites, or sold by relatives who needed money to survive. They may also have been created with honorable intentions. If anyone who views these photos can provide information regarding the people's identity, I ask that they contact the publisher, so that the names may be added to the captions.

Miigwetch to Susan Wyman of Wyman House Publications, Ann Arbor, for her help with pre-format.

CONTENTS

FIRST STONE
"WHO IS ANISHNAUBEK?" 1

"WHAT IS MAINSTREAM CULTURE?" 2
"WHY WERE EUROPEAN AND NATIVE CULTURES SO DIFFERENT?" ...4
"DO THE ANISHINAABEG HAVE A CULTURE?" 6

SECOND STONE
"WHERE IS ANISHINAUBEK FROM?" 8

"HOW CAN A SPOKEN WORD HAVE POWER?" 10
"WHAT DOES "ANISHINAABE" MEAN?" 11
"WHAT IS THE REAL ANISHINAABE STORY?" 15

THIRD STONE
"WHAT MAKES THE ANISHINAABE WAY?" 17

"WHAT IS SPECIAL ABOUT ANISHINAABE HOMES?" 18
"HOW DID ANISHINAUBEK LEARN THEIR VALUES?" 20
"WHAT DID ANISHINAUBEK GROW IN THEMSELVES?" 24
"WHAT IS NATURAL TIME?" 26

FOURTH STONE
"HOW WAS ANISHINAABE CULTURE ORGANIZED?" ..27

"DID THE ANISHINAABEG HAVE CHIEFS?" 30
"WHAT IS AN ANISHINAABE COUNCIL?" 31
"WHAT HAPPENED TO ANISHINAABEG WHO MISBEHAVED?" 34

FIFTH STONE
"WHAT DOES ANISHINAUBEK KNOW ABOUT LIFE?" .37

"HOW DID ANISHINAUBEK PUT SPIRIT TOGETHER WITH SCIENCE?" .39
"COULD ANISHINAUBEK REALLY TALK WITH PLANTS, ROCKS, AND ANIMALS?" 43
"WHY WAS ANISHINAUBEK SPEAKING TO THE DIRECTIONS?" 45
"WHY COULDN'T THE EUROPEANS ACCEPT ANISHINAABE IDEAS?" . .48

SIXTH STONE
"WHAT KINDS OF CEREMONY DID ANISHINAUBEK HAVE?" 50

"WHAT WAS A VISION SEEKING CEREMONY?" 51
"ABOUT THE SACRED PIPE" .54

SEVENTH STONE
"HOW DID ANISHINAUBEK MAINTAIN GOOD HEALTH?" . .59

"WHAT IS A PURIFICATION LODGE?" 60
"IS A MADOOTIZOON LIKE A SAUNA?" 62
"HOW DID ANISHAUBEK HEAL THOSE WHO WERE ILL OR INJURED?" 64
"WHAT DID A "MEDICINE MAN" REALLY DO?" 65
"HOW DOES ANISHINAUBEK BECOME TRAINED IN HEALING?" 68

LAST STONE
"HOW IS ANISHINAABE CULTURE TODAY?" 70

"HOW DID THE GOVERNMENTS TRY TO CHANGE ANISHINAUBEK?" . .73
"HOW HAS ANISHINAUBEK TRIED TO FIT WITH MAINSTREAM CULTURE?" .77
"WHAT IS A "POW-WOW?" 78

FIRST STONE
"WHO IS ANISHINAUBEK?"

When you walk through the halls of your school, you may be passing students who are Native American. You might not know it, because they might look slightly African, or Asian, or Mexican. They might even look Caucasian, if they only have one grandparent who is Native American. If you live in the Great Lakes area of the United States or Canada, these students are likely to be Ojibway, Odawa, or Potawatomi. Those three tribes are all related, by the name Anishinaabe (Ah-nish-un-ah-bay). This book is about differences between Anishinaabe culture and the cultures of the other people who came to live in this area.

A Circle of Stones -

A "culture" is created from many ways that a group of people like to live together. You may have learned some things about native cultures in younger grades, maybe about their houses, their clothing and crafts, and their leaders. But a culture also is made from ideas people believe about where they came from, and why. It is made of ideas about how everyone ought to get along together, and how to help those who are not so healthy or happy. It is made of styles and art, of dancing and song, stories, and tradition. Especially, it is woven, like a blanket, into language.

Anishinaabe culture is different because it places value, or importance on different ways of feeling, thinking, and being, than the ways of "mainstream" culture.

"WHAT IS MAINSTREAM CULTURE?"

Mainstream culture is what is popular in society. It is what most people like to believe is the best way to think, and behave. Mainstream culture in the United States comes from many sources. Part of it comes from the cultures of the Europeans who first came to the Americas. Part of it comes from the cultures of the Africans who were brought to the Americas, and their descendents who have created their own culture. Other parts come from cultures of the Middle Eastern countries, and Asian countries. Finally, some parts come from Native American culture, including South and Central American, and Alaskan Native. Did you know that the idea of using balls in games, and the idea of using teams in sports, both were introduced by Native Americans?

Popular sports are part of mainstream culture. Popular fashions and styles, music, language, jokes, all are part of mainstream culture. In the United States, it is more popular to belong to one of the two main political parties, and to be Christian in one's beliefs. It is especially popular in the United States to have money. It is popular to have a steady job with regular hours and a regular pay check. It is popular to gain status in one's job and become a manager for others. It is also popular in the United States to buy and own "things" with one's money, especially "new things".

There may be nothing wrong with these values, but they are very different from traditional values held by Anishinaabe people. When mainstream culture takes the view that others outside the mainstream are "less fortunate", or "disadvantaged", or "uncivilized", racism begins to happen. Often, people who want to be part of the mainstream decide to be mean to the others, or try to send them away somewhere. Sometimes they try to force the others to become part of the mainstream. You might see this happen in Middle School, where some students are "cool" and others are "nerds" or "freaks". It takes courage to find your own way to respect all people.

A Circle of Stones -

Above Illustration. "The Artists of Being Alive."
By J. Stone. Silverton, Oregon.

"WHY WERE EUROPEAN AND NATIVE CULTURES SO DIFFERENT?"

Anthropologists are scientists who study how cultures are special, and how they change. These kinds of scientists are trained to make guesses about how and why things happened, and then to try to prove their guesses right. There have been many books written to explain how British, French, other European cultures changed. Some writers think ancient ancestors of Ireland and Scotland, the Celtic people, and ancestors of the East European countries, the Slavic people, lived in tribal ways, with similar values and beliefs as Anishinaabek. Those writers base their guesses partly on letters written by commanders of Roman armies that came to take over the tribal people.

No one seems to know why the leaders of Rome, who were learning from the culture of the ancient Greek people, who in turn were learning from the cultures of other areas around the Mediterranean Sea decided that their culture was the best. But they had found a way to put their language into printing, and had great thinkers who wrote books about Roman values. They created an army large enough to win over most of the European continent and northern Africa. To all of these areas the Romans took their values and tried to force people to accept them.

If you take a World History class, you may learn more about Roman culture. It was one in which great ideas for building, organizing, and art were made. It also made popular the use of money, and jobs for earning pay. But Roman men had more power in their lives than Roman women. Women were not allowed to own houses, be leaders, or make important decisions. Roman culture also allowed people to "own" other people as slaves. In this way, two "core values" of Roman culture can be seen as ones which say: "Take control over what is outside you. Take power over others, before they take power over you."

I have heard some anthropologists say they think the environment where people live, the climate and type of land can make a big difference in the people's life style and beliefs. Around the Mediterranean Sea, there is so much good land for farming, many more people can be fed. With a greater number of people living more permanently in a large area, the ideas of owning land, and having power over other people could have become more popular. But there are examples of Native American cultures, such as the Mayan, Cherokee, Pueblo, and Eastern tribes which had a lot of people, grew plenty of food, and did not take up values like those of the

Romans.

Anishinaabe elders say their ancestors did not take on their values because of needing to survive with small groups of people in a difficult climate. They ask that their people be respected for their own history, passed down from elders for thousands of years. This story tells how the ancient ones received their values as gifts by listening to the voices of the plants, animals, earth, moon, sun, stars, and God.

"DO THE ANISHINAABEG HAVE A CULTURE?"

The Anishinaabeg have a culture that is many thousands of years old. They have a complicated language, and a balanced system of government with representatives from all parts of their society. They have their own popular styles of fashion, art, music, dance and games. They have their own religion, similar to other major religions of the world, with a "supreme being", and a "code of ethics" or ways to live a good, peaceful, and healthy life.

In the culture of Anishinaubek, it is popular to be an equal part of a group, instead of trying to get status. Power is something which comes from one's own inner beauty; and control is to be gained only over one's self. It is popular for them to have fewer "things", and to share what they do have. It is popular to live more for each moment, than for the future, or defined by a schedule. It is popular to learn for the sake of learning, and to respect all people, all cultures, and all of life. There are many good val-

-- First Stone

ues in Anishinaabe culture, just like there are in all cultures.

I have heard some young children say that there are no more "Indians" left in the world. This is not so. There are millions of Native people in America today. The culture of Anishinaubek is very much alive, and growing stronger every day. It is my hope that by reading this book, you will have more respect for Native culture, no matter who your ancestors were.

Illustration. Traditional Anishinaabe dolls.
Courtesy NAA/Smithsonian Institute.
596D37, 596D38

SECOND STONE
"WHERE IS ANISHINAUBEK FROM?"

In our present time, most people in Anishinaabe communities speak English. Ojibway language is taught at some colleges, and schools which are near Native communities. In many places, Native language is becoming more popular.

When you meet someone who is Anishinaabe, you may like to say "hello" in their language. You may say, "Buzheau" (buh-jeau), or "Aniin" (ah-nee). After saying "hello", they may ask, "Where are you from?" In their language this might be, "En dayan" (ehn-dai-yun). It usually means more than, "Where do you live?" Often it is a question which asks where you were raised, maybe which reservation, or which village. It might also be asking about which 'clan' you might be from, or which 'band'. A 'clan' includes all a person's relatives on either their father or mother's side of the family. A 'band' includes the families in a certain area. I have noticed, when Anishinaabe people speak at a meeting, they first say their name, then their clan, and often which band or reservation they are from. By European custom, a person had a "surname" which used to contain information about their family occupation, or town of origin.

    Finding an answer to the question, "Where are the Anishinaabe, as a People, from?" is more difficult. Anthropologists have their guesses. Many think Native Americans are related to people who traveled over an ancient "land bridge" from the Asian continent. Anishinaabe elders say these ideas do not respect their people, or their culture. The elders know an ancient story in which the ancestors of Native people sent their spirit selves to Earth from the stars. These "star beings" are said to have come to help the ordinary "two legged" live in peace, and to honor all life with prayer. As this knowledge is shared by the old ones, passed down through generations for thousands of years, and is shared by many of the North American Tribes, the elders wonder why anthropologists will not accept this knowledge as truth.

A Circle of Stones -

"HOW CAN A SPOKEN WORD HAVE POWER?"

If you have any doubt about how strong a word can be, just think of how you feel when someone swears at you. In my meetings with Anishinaabe elders, some asked how it could be good to write sacred knowledge as "fact" in a book. "When it is fact it no longer breathes, and no longer has a heartbeat," they said. "Our children were taught by stories that were told. That way they could get the deeper meaning." The elders have given permission for me to write what is in this book, because they feel it is important at this time for more of the world's children to know about Native culture.

The people called Ojibway, Odawa, and Potowatomi are now spread over an area from the northeast of United States and Canada, to areas west of Minnesota and midwestern Canada. The stories of where they first began, and how they traveled, were sometimes drawn in pictures on large pieces of birchbark. These are called "scrolls". There is a book I have seen which tells about the scrolls, and the elders who keep them.

But the stories told by the elders to explain pictures on the scrolls, or any other story of the past, are often different from area to area. Sometimes the reason for differences in the stories was, that an elder may only know the story as far back as the start of the travels somewhere along the way. When you hear an elder tell a story, they usually will end by saying, "That is how it was told to me." Often they will say who told it to them. It is also like this with the meanings and spellings of Anishinaabe words, which vary throughout parts of Ontario, Michigan, Wisconsin, and Minnesota.

"WHAT DOES 'ANISHINAABE' MEAN?"

The word "Anishinaabe" is said to have a number of meanings. To some elders, it means "From where first man was lowered". This refers to the ancient story of the "star beings". To other elders, "Anishinaabe" means "People who come from where the sun rises." This comes from a part of Anishinaabe history, in which many of the people moved away from the Great Lakes to look for the "Land of the Dawn". Those people traveled all the way to the Atlantic Ocean, and stayed for hundreds of years. After the Viking explorers sailed to this continent from Scandanavia, bringing disease and war, many of the Anishinaabe living by the sea coast decided to return on a long journey back to the Great Lakes. The elders call this the Great Migration, or "Kitchi Goziwin" (Keech Gau-zih-win). There are some who hear "Anishinaabe" to mean "The Good People", while others who use it to denote an "Indian person" in general. In this book, we use "Anishinaabe" to describe someone who is a member of the three "brother" tribes—Ojibway, Odawa, and Potowatomi.

A Circle of Stones -

"Stopping to give thanks."
From an original lithograph.

Basil Johnston, a respected Ojibway author and elder from Northern Ontario, shared with me his views on the varying styles of language within Anishinaabe culture. He said it would be improper to divide the Anishinaabe people into parts, such as "Eastern speaking" and "Western speaking", since the language remains "one language" which lives within "one culture".

Mr. Johnston also cleared up a misunderstanding regarding the terms "Algonquin" and "Algonkian". For many years, historians have used the term "Algonquin" when referring to the Anishinaabeg who lived in the northeast part of the continent at the time the French explorers arrived. The word "Algonkian" has been used as a name for their language.

Mr. Johnston explains these terms were invented by the French. He suggests we acknowledge "Anishinaubae" as the true name of the people, and "Anishinaubaemoowin" as the term for their language. Notice that Mr. Johnston prefers to use the "au" and "ae" and double "oo" in his spelling. The double "oo" is spoken as a long "o", as in "boat".

There are differing ideas about origins of the names used by the "Brother Tribes". Some writers have heard the name "Ojibway" meant, "People with beaded shoes". I have heard it said that the names "grew" from terms describing the tasks people had during Kitchi Goziwin. It is said that those who kept the scrolls safe, came to be known as "Ojibway". The name "Odawa" is thought to mean "traders", describing the skill those people had in trading during the journey. "Potowatomi" is believed to have meant "keepers of the fire", due to the responsibility held by those people for keeping coals from each night's fire live for the next night. This view of the names grants each of the "Brother Tribes" an important role to insure the survival of the people. Mr. Johnston takes another view, that the tribes probably developed their names earlier than Kitchi Goziwin; and that

A Circle of Stones -

responsibilities for the scrolls, for trade, and keeping of live coals were shared among, and within all three tribes.

Ojibway Beaded Velvet Moccasins.
Late 19th Century. Red Lake.
Courtesy of Minnesota Historical Society.

--- Second Stone

"WHAT IS THE REAL ANISHINAABE STORY?"

The real story is best told by Ojibway authors such as Eddie Benton-Benai, and Basil Johnston. It is a story full of wonder, magic, and lessons for living in honor of all life. It begins with God, called "Great Mystery", who sends a dream out to the end of the universe. It includes a great flood, which destroys the first humans, after which a great turtle works with other brave animals to create land, on which new humans may arrive. It further explains how those new humans learned from the animals how to survive, to have wisdom, and to care for one another. There are parts which describe how the people found their way back to the Great Lakes in Kitchi Goziwin, following a shell which floated in the air; and how they began to harvest black rice. There are other parts which tell how the first clans were started, and how medicine, healing, and ways to pray came to the people. Many in mainstream culture think of these stories as interesting "myths", or "folk tales". If these people were to sit, wrapped in a blanket, in a winter longhouse late at night; if they were to listen to the story, told through the dancing of fire shadows—they might feel the stories begin to breathe, to come alive with a deep truth of their own.

A Circle of Stones -

Anishinaabe women gathering black rice.
From original lithograph.

THIRD STONE
"WHAT IS THE ANISHINAABE *WAY*?"

You may have already learned in school books some facts about how the Great Lakes Anishinaabeg lived long ago. If you are Anishinaabe, you may remember your elders telling about traditional times, when the People lived in dome-shaped homes made of saplings and tree bark, and traveled on the rivers and lakes in canoes. But most of those books do not tell much about why the People chose to live as they did, even when European families began to build log and stone homes nearby. Of course many Anishinaabe families liked to start using European cloth, beads, tools, pots, and other useful items. But there were reasons for living in simple round homes, with thin walls, and woven grass mats for the floors.

If you think about how many thousands of people in America like to camp in tents for vacation, you start to understand. If you have enjoyed camping yourself, you might have noticed it was because you felt more free to "be yourself". You probably felt more free from worries about time, and having to dress and behave in certain ways because "society" expects it. You might have started to feel more happy , and naturally started to treat others with more kindness. If you had a bad experience, fighting with weather, insects, poison ivy, and other parts of nature, it was probably because you were fighting against becoming more "natural". But if you can become more and more "natural", you start to love more and more of what is natural around you.

"WHAT IS SPECIAL ABOUT ANISHINAABE HOMES?"?

Anishinaabe elders tell me their ancestors' homes, and life style were very natural. They say part of natural order is the circle. The Ojibway of Northern Ontario say "geewitau-ayauwin" for "circular". Round and ball-shaped objects and forms can be found everywhere in nature. In the same way, the growing of life goes in stages which make a circle, and is called a "cycle". This is "wauweeyaawin". You may have learned about the cycles of water, heat, and carbon in earth sciences books. So it is with birth, childhood, adulthood, and old age. I learned from Adam Fortunate Eagle Nordwall, a very respected elder, writer, and artist, that the frame of the Ojibway "wiigiwaum" (wee-jih-wahm) home was made with arches and hoops which were symbols of cycles in nature. Doors always faced east, allowing morning light to come in. Family members then could step out toward the place of "enlightenment", as morning is a symbol for "birth of light in the body". Sapling hoops wrap clockwise around, thick end to thin end, to create a motion of growth, each hoop a symbol for one stage of life.

Wiigiwaum. Mille Lacs.
Courtesy Minnesota Historical Society.

Living in a home which is made in "alignment", or to go together with natural order, creates a special feeling in the people who live in that way. It is not so unusual, either. The old Romans thought they were "aligning" their buildings with the way their gods and goddesses lived. Ancient

A Circle of Stones -

Japanese people had a similar way of "aligning" parts of their homes with elements of nature called "feng shui". In an Anishinaabe wiigiwaum, a fire would burn in the center, with smoke rising out a hole in the top. Adam taught me how the people would honor and give thanks to God for the fire, by holding a pinch of tobacco up, saying a prayer, and then gently giving the tobacco to the fire. Each person entering would perform this prayer, then walk sun-wise around the fire toward their place.

"HOW DID ANISHINAUBEK LEARN THEIR VALUES?"

Can you imagine living in one room with maybe a brother and sister, an uncle, mother and father, and a grandmother? I learned there were usual places for family members in a wiigiwaum, and some important "norms", which are like "gentle" rules reminding everyone to treat one another with kindness. For example, the west part was usually reserved for the "elders", the grandparents. They were honored in many ways. Elders would be served first at meals. Children were taught to speak softly around them, and to listen when they spoke.

Adam taught me that babies, when they were first born, would be given a name by an elder. The parents would ask an elder to find a special name. The elder would hold the baby up to the sky, toward the places of the four winds, and tell the baby's name to the ancestors and the world of spirit. In future times, when this young one would pray, the world of spirit would know his or her name, and respond. A baby, called "abinoodjeehnse" (ah-bin-oh-jeen-say) in most Ojibway communities, then spent its early daytimes tucked in a bundle on its mother's back. I imagine this allowed a baby to feel the wonders of nature, while also feeling secure.

Of course, Anishinaabe people are human, and not without human emotions—jealousy, sadness, anger included. When I spend some time among Anishinaabe friends, I usually find a lot of teasing. But again, there were norms, ways of helping to keep life quiet. When children might step out of line, say something rude, the elders say there were no harsh words, no loud voices, no spanking or hitting by the parents. Instead, an aunt or uncle or elder might be asked to speak with the child. When adults stepped on the rights of others, a "council", a specially chosen circle of leaders, helped to find a solution. You can read more about "councils" in a later chapter.

Another strong Anishinaabe value which probably helped people get along well was that of cleanliness, called "biin-iziwin" (been-ih-zih-win), and order. Alton Sonny Smart, and Ojibway teacher and healer from Wisconsin, taught me about this. It was so strong that some elders remember a grandfather getting them up for daily morning baths in a lake or river, even when they had to chop a hole in the ice. Women who were known for their tidiness in housekeeping, and weaving of fine grass mats for their floors were preferred by men for marriage.

A Circle of Stones -

Ojibway abinoodjehnse. Class Lake, 1915
Courtesy Minnesota Historical Society.

    The value placed on being generous is one I have experienced often in my contact with Anishinaabe culture. Always on my visits I am welcomed warmly, offered food and a place in their activity. There are so many parts of Anishinaabe tradition which add to their people's culture—the styles of hunting, fishing, craft, games, and songs: the festivals held at seasonal times to celebrate harvesting berries, rice, or maple sugar. Gambling games were so much a part of ancient Native culture that there were songs made especially for those games. But there is plenty about these parts of Anishinaabe life in other books. What the elders feel most important, is for you to know about the Anishinaabe "Way". Sometimes this is called "The Red Road" or "The Path of Life". It is all about living life in alignment with the order of nature, and includes those "values", "ethics", and "norms" about which we have been learning.

"Shield of Self Respect" By Steve Chensue

"WHAT DID ANISHINAUBEK GROW IN THEMSELVES?"

There is another value to talk about in this chapter. It is "respect". In Northern Ontario the term for this is: "mino-audjiwaewin" (mih-no au-jee-way-win). This is a very important value to traditional Native culture. It also was the root of much misunderstanding between the Native and European cultures.

The elders say, in traditional times, the children were taught that humans are not the true owners of anything—even their own body. It was taught that their body was simply a slower vibration of light, slow enough that it can be seen and felt. But it was said a person is like one "cell" of God, and that God is the true owner of life, and light. This way of teaching places responsibility inside each human being for all of his or her relating to all other parts of nature. The elders explain that it also opens the way for us to consider all parts of nature not only alive, but related to us.

For some reason, European culture started long ago to have in it the threat of being punished for acts of disrespect. Starting back in Egyptian times, and Greek and Roman times, people were supposed to respect the leaders, and rules, and gods, or they would be punished. What children learn from this way, is that they are separate from God, that they own all parts of nature, and that respect is forced upon them. By the time the first Europeans came to North America, they had become so separate from nature, and so afraid of it, that people found using plants for healing, or symbols of natural order were called a "witch" and were often killed. Bathing had become unpopular because being naked was thought to be "evil". People even thought that dancing to drum sounds would bring "devils" out of the ground.

Basil Johnston informed me "mino-audjiwaewin" means: "to honor another in act, not only in mind". He suggested that "mino-audjiwaewin" is nurtured in children by good parenting. When parents honor their children's freedom, and teach them self-respect, respect for life then follows. A child who is often punished, is likely to have trouble knowing who they are, except as a body which feels pain and anger. One who knows only pain and anger,

Ojibway Pow-Wow participants Randy Patterson,
Iron Worker, and son Cam.

will have difficulty recognizing beauty, or respecting it.

Anthropologists form theories about how values grow in cultures as a way for the people to deal with their environment. Another misunderstanding Basil Johnston helped clarify, is that Anishinaabe values did not grow as a way to "adapt" or deal with life. They "did not need a circle to instill in them equality", he said. It is common for a Native person to thank a tree, or a river, or an animal for giving something valuable—such as it's life. This way of thinking is not "primitive". It is not "evil". It is what comes naturally, when one lives naturally, and nurtures respect within themself.

"WHAT IS "NATURAL TIME"?

The Anishinaabe "Way" is like a "code" of good ways to be with one's self; and toward life and others. The elders say the Path of Life has been passed along to generations of children for thousands of years, in a gentle, soft spoken style. It keeps Anishinaubek walking with feet strongly connected to the earth. It makes Anishinaubek able to move in alignment with the earth's time—that is, natural time. Most of us live according to time kept by clocks. Natural time is the kind that tells you when you are finished with a meal, or when you are ready to wake up from a good night's sleep. If you pay attention to natural time, it can tell you just when to call your girlfriend, and when to study for a test. When you feel natural time, it is much easier to learn another important Anishinaabe value—patience!

FOURTH STONE
"HOW WAS ANISHINAABE CULTURE ORGANIZED?"

The very first Anishinaabeg, the elders say, had brought with them from the stars the knowing of how to love and care for one another in strong ways. But they were new to the earth, and to having these kinds of bodies. So it is said that the animals helped them learn to survive. Some learned from the otter and wolf how to fish and hunt. Some learned from the bear how to guard the children. Others learned from the deer about music and poetry. A few learned from the turtle, the ways of healing with plants. A few others learned from the fish about teaching and learning. Those small groups are said to have accepted the spirit teach-

A Circle of Stones

ing of the animal to which they felt the most natural connection, and borrowed the name of this animal as a kind of "title" for their relatives, called a "clan".

The Ojibway term for "clan" is "doodem". In one popular way of spelling Anishinaabe words, two vowels are put together to make a special vowel sound. The "o" sound in doodem sounds like "doe". Over many thousands of years, the number of doodemwin grew and changed. They became a way to make natural order among the many branches of Anishinaabe families. It became "custom", that children born would be naturally part of their father's doodem. But when a young woman married, she could keep her own doodem. Members of a doodem were like cousins in European culture. Young people are not allowed to marry someone of their same doodem.

It is not a rule that you would have to be a fighter if you are born into the doodem of Mukwa, the Bear. You might have more feeling for hunting or making songs. Then perhaps you might pray about this, and get an answer that you should ask to be "adopted" into another doodem. In modern times, of course there are no doodemwin for steelworking, or driving a bulldozer. But among those Anishinaabeg with whom I have spoken, there still is a connection they feel with their doodem, and a sense of pride.

– Fourth Stone

Circle of Ojibway Doodemwin.
Arrangement by Author.

A Circle of Stones -

"DID THE ANISHINAABEG HAVE CHIEFS?"

The elders tell me there were no "chiefs" ruling the tribes like "kings". They say the word "chief" was used by the Europeans to describe some Anishinaabe leaders. As it was told to me, there also were originally two doodemwin for leadership, the Maang or Loon Doodem, and the Jiijaak or Crane Doodem. In Anishinaabe culture, it is important to have balance in leadership between creative thinking and stable thinking. An old legend tells how the special qualities of cranes and loons hold these kinds of thinking in balance. Cranes and loons are migrating birds—flying special places for winter like their friends, the geese. Of these migrating marsh birds, cranes are always the first to fly. In the legend, the loons get the cranes to let them go first for a change. The loons had a creative idea for flying "south" by a new route and caused everyone to become lost. Of course, now we know that loons go to the Atlantic Ocean to find mates.

I have heard in Native wisdom a saying: "Traditions should only last as long as they are useful." It is helpful to have those in government who can come up with fresh ideas. The cranes are symbols of the more stable part of leadership. They are the ones who can say whether a fresh idea makes good sense. Between the two parts is a middle agreement. Finding this middle aggreement takes flexibility, and maturity. It requires the ability to "compromise", where each person adjusts their view, in favor of a decision which may be best for everyone.

―――――――――――――――――――――――――――――――― Fourth Stone

"WHAT IS AN ANISHINAABE COUNCIL?"

In Anishinaabe culture, a council of leaders would meet to make important decisions. In Northern Ontario the term for such meetings is "geekittoowining" (gee-kih-to-win-ing). There would gather members from a variety of doodemwin, those who were highly respected. There would be those from the Maang and Jiijaak doodemwin. And there would be a person who was chosen to pray with the Sacred Pipe. You can learn more about Anishinaabe prayer in a later chapter. For now, it is good just to know that the Sacred Pipe only held tobacco or a mix of other plants--no drugs--and that the prayers, which were carried in the rising smoke, were helping the council to find, not only the middle agreement, but also to see how their decisions would affect their children, and grandchildren—seven generations into the future! This smoking of the Pipe was called "ziquswaediwining" (zih-qus-way-dih-win-ing).

It is important to remember that Anishinaabe councils would need to find that middle agreement, and have everyone's vote "yes" to be finished, even if it took three days or longer. So the Speaking Staff was passed from member to member, each one expressing their ideas and opinions. A Speaking Staff, I have been told, is usually made of wood, but has special animal fur, feathers, beads, or other objects attached. It is called "geekitto-wautik" (gee-kit-oh-wau-tik). It helped the speaker focus their thoughts, and others to focus their thoughts on the speaker. It also ensured that only truth would be spoken.

A Circle of Stones -

Photo of Speaking Staff.

The elders tell me the long time spent on decisions might have been one reason "treaties" between Native peoples and the North American governments were so often broken or never followed. Officials from the governments would invite members of the councils to meet and sign papers. I have seen copies of some of those papers. They are written in a confusing style. To make matters worse, whiskey and wine would be given to the council members. Some members would say they needed more time to think and would go home. The officials then offered the other council members fancy presents if they would sign the treaty. These members would sign, while the ones who had gone home said the treaty was no good, and told their clan members not to follow it.

By Anishinaabe custom, leaders were not supposed to make decisions without agreement from the councils. It could be in times of war a leader might "bend" this rule a bit. "Chief" Pontiac was an Odawa leader who brought together an army of Anishinaabe warriors to fight against British soldiers in the Great Lakes area, long before the Revolutionary War. He would pretend to bring presents into a British fort. His warriors would hide weapons under blankets, and surprise the British with an attack. His trick didn't work in Detroit, the last fort Pontiac tried, because the British heard about his secret. But even if "Chief" Pontiac had succeded in Detroit, his army was getting very tired of fighting. It was hard on the Anishinaabe familes to have the warriors gone, and hard on the warriors to be away from their communities for a long time. Pontiac, and many other brave Anishinaabe leaders, strove to balance the needs of their people for maintaining traditional culture, and adapting to pressure from the Europeans to change. It must have been quite a difficult job.

The way of the councils was lost in most Native communities when the governments of United States and Canada set aside land called "reservations" on which Anishinaabe families could live, and set up small "democratic" councils there, supervised by government workers. For some years, use of the Sacred Pipe was against government law, and whatever idea had more than half the votes would win. Now in many places, traditional style councils have again formed to make decisions for Native people, and the Pipe is again permitted.

"WHAT HAPPENED TO ANISHINAABEG WHO MISBEHAVED?"

There was quite a variety of decisions to be made in old times, as always, the elders say. There were decisions about where to hunt, and where to move the villages at season changes, so as to be closest to the herds of deer or elk. There were decisions about festivals and gatherings, marriages, funerals, and divorce. There were decisions about trade, change, and war. Always there was the work to find a middle agreement.

But running like a stream within a traditional council was another value of Anishinaubek: balance. The word for this in most Ojibway communities is "guyuksidigaewin" (guy-yuk-sid-ih-gay-win). I am told it means "to make things right". This is the kind of balance between giving and receiving. It is what happens in a good trade. It also happens when someone or some part of nature is being thanked or honored for what energy has been given.

Did you ever think to tell a tree what you need it for, and to ask it's permission to use it? Adam Fortunate Eagle told me about this. He said you will feel energy pushing at your hand on the trunk of the tree if it is ok. You will feel it pulling away if it is not ok. If the tree is ok to be used, and you cut it, then you put some tobacco on top of the stump and thank the tree for its "giveaway". If it is not ok, you don't cut it! I have tried this way, and found that it works.

There were times the councils had to restore balance when someone had done harm to another person or people. This was much different than "punishment". You might know about this if your mother ever told you to put a bandage on the scraped arm of your brother after you pushed your brother down. Saying you are "sorry" is only the first step to "making things right". The elders say that in old Native culture, a man who killed another member of his tribe or clan or village might have been told by the council to provide and care for the killed man's family for the rest of his life, including providing food, shelter, clothing—in addition to providing for his own family. It rarely happened that anyone would be asked to leave the tribe forever, as I am told, and only in a case where someone might have killed their own child or parent. Still, their life would not be taken directly from them. To Anishinaubek, life was a contract that should stay between each person and God.

Here is how an Ojibway leader looked in the nineteenth century, when the councils were working on treaties to sell Anishinaabe land to the United States government.

A Circle of Stones -

Ojibway leader.
Lithograph Courtesy Bentley Historical Library.

FIFTH STONE
"WHAT DOES ANISHINAUBEK KNOW ABOUT LIFE?"

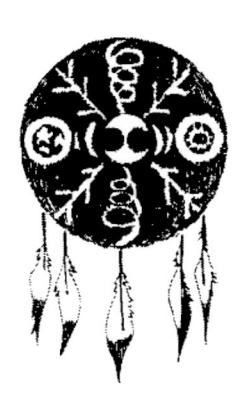

Some people have very strong beliefs. Some even will fight to defend their beliefs. Have you ever heard someone say, "I'll believe it when I see it"? Many people will only trust their experience. One wise elder once told me that "true knowledge is information that works, or is useful." Scientists try to prove an idea to be true by testing it. In Native culture, many ideas were tested by thousands of people over many thousands of years. As thousands of people found the same results, these ideas came to be accepted as "true knowledge". There is a word for this, used by those Anishinaabeg who live in Northern Ontario: "kikaendaussowin" (kih-

A Circle of Stones

kane-dow-so-win).

In Native culture, because of living so closely with nature, this "kikaendaussowin" had its source first in what was brought from the stars, then in what was learned from listening to the earth, and to all of the "children" of the earth. Kikaendaussowin is like a long and complicated "knowledge story", into which important facts are woven like designs into a blanket. Students of Anishinaabe medicine and healing spend years learning to understand the meanings of the designs. Some elders, like Adam Fortunate Eagle from Minnesota, and Sam Ozawamik (Brown Beaver) from Manitoulin Island, are great story tellers, who share parts of the "knowledge story" with groups of seekers and children. The story tellers and spiritual leaders of the Anishinaabe remind us that the "knowledge story" itself is alive, and remains alive as it is passed on orally.

In this part of our book, we must try to understand what Native people mean when they speak of the "spirit world". In order to do this we need to open our minds. Try to imagine you are lying in a grassy field in the middle of a great forest. There you can watch the clouds move across the sky, hear birds, and a river nearby. Imagine that the earth is a wonderful "mother", a real alive being, whose name in Anishinaabe language would be Akii, and start to speak to her. See if you feel some response from her coming into the middle part of your body. If you can trust that she is alive, then every part of nature becomes a relative to you. Trees then become the "standing nation". Rocks become "stone children". Animals become "little brother" or "little sister". When you start to see life in this way, you need never feel lonely when away from your friends and family.

HOW DID ANISHINAUBEK PUT "SPIRIT" TOGETHER WITH "SCIENCE"?

Traditional Anishinaubek, the elders say, believed that God created all forms of all things through having a great dream and making it become real. In this way, God is known as the one who gives "spirit energy" to all matter. The word for "God" commonly used is "Kitchi Manido" (Keech, or Kih-chee Mun-ih-doh). I have been taught that it means "Great Mystery", or "The Creator". Some people may think that Anishinaubek must have be praying to a different God than the One Christians call "God", because they don't say the same word. In modern times, there may be some Native people who do prefer to think of Kitchi Manido as being their very own God. The elders with whom I have spoken would disagree, saying this will only keep cultures at odds with one another. They say it is only the concept of God which may be different. In the Anishinaabe concept, Kitchi Manido is half male energy, and half female energy, since it takes both parts to create. What do you think?

But let's get back to speaking of "spirit energy". As it is told to me, this is partly the "life force" which keeps our heart beating and lungs breathing. Some people have a strong hold on their life force, with will power. They can be badly injured, and still hold on to life. Others let go of life quite easily. Modern science recognizes the presence of "life force", through studies of molecular and quantum physics. But most sci

A Circle of Stones -

Circle of elements and seasons, with traditional colors.
By Author.

entists would hesitate to accept the idea that "spirit energy" has an "awareness" which can "communicate" without the need of a body. In mainstream culture, there is some fascination with what is called "psychic talent". The elders tell me there is nothing so strange about relating with the "spirit world". Sure, they say, you have to know what you're doing. But "reading some one's mind" is just an extension of learning to have compassion, to feel how they might feel.

In order to give you just a peak into the world of kikaendaussowin, the elders have permitted me to share a few small parts of the "knowledge story" of Anishinaubek.

Fifth Stone

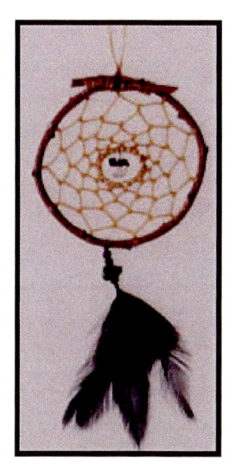

Photo of a "Dream Catcher".

It is said that Kitchi Manido gives Akii a special job to do every day, every minute—to change "spirit energy" into "substance energy", light into life, on her surface. In order to do her job, Akii uses four helpers, the elements which are a part of her. Earth is a strong helper. It is always there when you need a foundation, a structure on which to build a home or a life or an idea. Water is a nourishing helper, which cleans and helps the flow of life, of changes, and feelings. Air is essential as a helper for our brains. We need oxygen to survive, and winds to remind us to be flexible with our minds. Fire is a very intense helper. It brings us light, warmth, and energy to move our machines. But fire also helps things to expand, like air heated up in a balloon. So we could say that fire also helps us as humans to stretch the limits of our awareness of spirit.

In the next part of the knowledge story, Akii gives birth to her four types of "children". First, come her mineral children, then her plant children, animal children, and finally her human children. To each, according to the elders, Kitchi Manido has given special ways to use energy. Think about this.

A Circle of Stones

Remember how a sidewalk stays warm long after night has cooled the air. Mineral children hold, "minjiimin" (min-jee-min). Think of the softness given by grasses, so many foods given by vegetables, beauty and scent given by flowers; and wood, shade and oxygen given by trees—all without expecting anything in return. Plant children give, "miigiwe" (mee-gih-way). In nature, animals take in to their lives with balance and care, all that is given. You are not likely to see "wild" animals getting fat, or developing weird habits, as our pets, or animals in captivity do. The animal children receive, "odapin" (oh-dah-pin). We humans are given the power of "dominion", the power to decide from our "free will", to either protect or destroy ourselves and the other children. We determine, "wawaenaadan" (wuh-wayn-ah-duhn).

It is often said in textbooks, that Native people did not waste anything they used from nature. The elders look at mainstream culture, and see huge amounts of waste. But they also see so many humans ignoring the lessons of Akii's other children. They see men hold in their emotions and become ill. They see women receive with their bodies and become obese. These are ways people fall out of connection with natural "spirit energy". We will talk more about this in the chapter on maintaining good health.

--- Fifth Stone

"COULD ANISHINAUBEK REALLY TALK WITH PLANTS, ROCKS, AND ANIMALS?"

In addition to being given a "spirit energy" by God, the elders say each of Akii's children were given a place on the "Circle of Life". The power given to each of the children was really their beauty given freely for all parts of the family to experience. So if you want to talk with a plant, you align the part of you which is like a plant's energy—the flowing giving part, your emotions—with the energy of the plant. Plants show us how to have trust in ourselves.

Suppose you want to talk to a rock! You align the part of you which is part of the mineral children—the holding part, your bones—and slow down your mind, your blood, every moving part of yourself so your life force moves slowly, like a rock. You might ask a question about ancient times, since rocks are so old, and listen for an answer to come through your bones.

It is not so difficult to speak with an animal, especially tame ones, since animals can understand our voice messages with their instinct feelings. Since my wife is an "animal whisperer", I have seen many examples in which she asks permission of an animal to help it, and explains in a normal voice to the animal what she wants to do. Animals which might have been very afraid, or could have hurt her, have become very calm when her intent is explained. Animals are here, the elders teach, to show us how to have balance and harmony in our lives. "Balance" means not to have too much, or too little; not to do too much or too little—how to be just right with ourselves and others. "Harmony" means to have the natural part of ourselves be at peace with the natural part of others.

A Circle of Stones -

Shield of Balance and Harmony.
By Author.

Looking at the beauty of Akii's children may help us remember that the races of humanity make up their own circle. On a circle, no part is more important to the movement of the "wheel" than any other part—each part plays its role. The elders ask us to remember that fear and distrust of other races only comes from not knowing enough about why cultures are different from one another. In traditional times, it was taught that there were four main races of human, each having their place on the four directions circle. Many elders stay with this teaching, but others welcome the more modern idea that there are no true "races" based on skin color any more in the world. They say there is still a circle of humans, but with as many shades of color as there are people. What do you think?

"WHY WAS ANISHNAUBEK SPEAKING TO THE DIRECTIONS?"

In the Anishinaabe way, it was Kitchi Manido who gave to all parts of nature seven "direction places" on their own inner Circle of Life. In this way, the Universe itself, and each star, each planet, each person, animal, plant, and stone also has seven direction places in how they relate to all other parts of nature. Each piece of dust or cell of life—even an idea has seven direction places. This may be a difficult concept to grasp. I will speak of the concept only in as much depth as I am permitted. This is because the concept itself is given "spirit energy" by The Creator, and is therefore "alive". In Anishinaabe culture, one must know a thing that is "alive" very thoroughly, before being permitted to speak of its nature. Then, one must use extreme caution in writing this knowledge, because "nailing it down" as "hard fact" takes life from it, as we have said before.

It has been important in traditional Native culture, to learn to connect with the "spirit energy" of the directions, because they can provide guidance in one's life, just as the elements and children of Akii also do. Anishinaabe spiritual leaders from different areas each have their own way of addressing the directions. Hap McCue uses terms which translate roughly to:

Mother Earth, Father Sky, and the Dwelling Places of the Four Winds. Members of the Anishinaabe religious society of Midewewin include a seventh direction, which translates generally as: Purpose and Meaning felt with the Heart.

It is said that the "spirit energy" of the directions sends beauty through symbols, seen and interpreted by those who connect with it in prayer. You may find different colors and meanings attributed to a circle of life by spiritual teachers from one Anishinaabe community, compared with those attributed to the circle in another community. The traditional colors used by Ojibway to signify the Dwelling Places of the Four Winds were Green, Red, Black, and White. The colors had strong meaning related to aspects of daily and seasonal life in a northern temperate climate. Colors used by many Odawa communities living farther south, were different, because their orientation to the "spirit energy" of the directions was different. In more recent times, some Anishinaabe leaders have begun to use the colors and symbolism of the plains tribes, as these attributes may speak to them with a beauty they find meaningful in their lives at this time.

— Fifth Stone

"Shield Of The Four Directions".
Painting by Susan Seddon Boulet.
C The Susan Eleanor Boulet Trust

    I have found it still customary for many Anishinaabeg to show appreciation daily to the directions for what they give to life. This is not "worshipping gods" or "devils" or anything of the kind. It is a way of staying connected with the "spirit energy" of that which Kitchi Manido created. When most of us go to a friend's house, and ask for a glass of water, we ask our friend, not God, for the water. In the same way, we may ask the North wind to send wisdom or strength. You may like to read more about how the Spirit Dwelling Places of the Four Winds were discovered by the sons of Nanabush, in <u>The Mishomis Book,</u> by Eddie Benton-Benai.

"WHY COULDN'T THE EUROPEANS ACCEPT ANISHINAABE IDEAS?"

Historians say, after the ancient visits from Vikings, the first Europeans to meet the Anishinaabe tribes were the French. There were traders, who traded many things made in Europe for animal furs and other things made by people of the Ojibway, Odawa, and Potowatomi. Soon after came the Jesuit Christian missionaries with strong beliefs that Anishinaabe ways of living and thinking were "evil". Since the time when the Roman armies took over Europe, and forced Christian beliefs onto the tribal people there, most Europeans had forgotten their own ways of relating to the earth as a "Mother", or honoring the circles and cycles of nature. They could not imagine Kitchi Manido as the same God to whom they prayed, and were too deeply afraid to change their awareness to a new level.

Another big problem was the language "barrier". Some of the traders and missionaries were able to learn some Anishinaabe language. But there were no televisions with satellite dishes, no radio talk shows, and few newspapers. Even if there had been newspapers, few of the people moving to the Great Lakes area around 1810 could have read them, since there were few schools. There was no way for people to learn about the gentle, spiritual ways of Anishinaabe culture. They were not even aware the Anishinaabeg had "ideas" about life, or words to express them.

A third big problem was greed and impatience of the new American culture after the Revolutionary War. People saw many ways to make money by selling land; selling trees for furniture, houses, boats, and paper; selling coal, salt, and copper. People didn't want to find out what Anishinaabe culture was about. Churches and governments joined together to say Native culture was "primitive", "against God", and should be "destroyed". Most people's attitude seemed to be: "OK! Just get them out of our way!"

From the 1830's to the 1930's, there were many attempts made by mainstream society to destroy Native culture. We will speak more of this in the last chapter. But for now, you should know that during that time, Native children in both United States and Canada were forced by the government to attend Christian schools, where they had to live, separated from their families for most of the year. They were forced to cut their hair, speak English, and wear European style clothes. Elders such as Basil Johnston, Sonny Smart, and Hap McCue have told about Native students being hit with sticks if they were caught speaking their own language, singing, or praying in their own way. These schools created a deep sense of shame in Anishinaabe children about their culture.

Lines of Anishinaabe children at Christian boarding school near Mt. Pleasant, Michigan. Courtesy, Clarke Historical Library.

SIXTH STONE
"WHAT KINDS OF CEREMONY DID ANISHINAUBEK HAVE?"

    Hap McCue, Ojibway elder and teacher from Ontario Canada has said that, even as he was a boy on a reserve, the whole life of each person was a ceremony. I imagine this to mean the people held in their mind, body, and spirit a constant attitude of prayer. "Attitude" can be positive or negative. Having a positive attitude means you are looking for the good side of everything. With a negative attitude you are looking for the bad side in all that you experience. An attitude of prayer is a positive one, with which you feel blessed by life and thankful for all that comes to you. But perhaps we should talk about what makes a "ceremony".

    A "ceremony" can be a simple act, called a "ritual"; or a series of acts performed in a special way. An example of ritual is the placing of a pinch of tobacco in the fire when entering one's home. All ceremonies are made to show honor and respect. Some, like those made to honor winners at the Olympics, or heroes in war are respecting the unusual braveness and strength those people found in themselves. Other ceremonies are made to honor a spiritual change in a person's life, such as birth, marriage, death, or becoming a young adult. Each culture has religious ceremonies which honor these events in their own way. Traditional Anishinaabe culture included all these ceremonies, and many others.

"WHAT WAS A VISION-SEEKING CEREMONY?"

The word used by Northern Ontario Ojibway for "ceremony" is megooshaewin (may-go-shay-win). We have spoken earlier about megooshaewinun for naming babies. Perhaps you would like to know somethng about megooshaewinun done by Anishinaabe children to honor their becoming a young adult. The elders say that when boys and girls start wanting to fall in love with each other, it is then time for them to make a megooshaewin to look for their own special meaning in life. This meaning is all about what your real beauty is as a person, what is truly great about you that you were born to give to the world. In Northern Wisconsin, the Ojibway call this "wenjii" (wayn-jee).

In Anishinaabe tradition, it is felt the best way to learn about one's wenjii is to spend time alone fasting and praying. A "fast" is when a person goes for some time without food, or even without food and water. Adam Fortunate Eagle once told me that one needs to make space in one's self for a "vision" to enter their body, and there isn't enough space if it's all full of food. Of course he was using some good Anishinaabe humor, but fasting is known in many cultures as a way to change one's awareness to a more spiritual level.

A ME-GOOSHAEWIN FOR YOU

Let's pretend you were going to make a "vision seeking" megooshaewin. We will pretend it is in the way told to me by those who know it from Northern Michigan.

For maybe a whole year before it is supposed to happen, you and one of your parents, father if you're a boy, mother if you're a girl, have been making together little gifts to give to those members of your family and clan that you want to "sponsor you" in your time alone. These will be people you love and trust, who will come at certain times to sing and pray for you while you seek your vision.

A few days before you are to start your megooshaewin, your parent prepares for you a little dome shaped shelter in the woods. An elder or medicine priest blesses the shelter with cedar and sweetgrass, so it is clean from any negative attitude energy. When all is ready, the family and sponsors come together to send you on your way.

The sacred pipe is filled with tobacco, smoked, and kept together by an elder or medicine priest to hold all the beauty of nature, and energy of

Kitchi Manido safe for you to use during your seeking. Then, maybe some color from earth or plants is applied to your face to let all nature know you are coming to seek a vision. Finally, a special song is sung as you go with some water and a blanket into the dark, secret space of the shelter.

At first, you only feel excited, and warmed by the support shown to you by your family and sponsors. For some time your mind floats from picture to picture, sometimes stopping for awhile to dream about a girl or boy you especially like. You start to hear night sounds, and notice how silly your mind is to be making thoughts about so many things. At some time you hear singing outside. You start to feel a bit sleepy and decide to try singing to stay awake. It is important to stay awake as long as possible so that the dream world and waking world get mixed together. Slowly, your mind starts to experience things which are strange. Your lose track of time, and pictures seem to appear in the shelter as real. A big brown bear seems to be walking right into the shelter, then flies strait up into the sky and makes a rainbow there. You hear singing far away, but you know it must be the sponsors.

Next thing you know, the shelter is opened, and you are greated by the smiles and hugs of family and sponsors. It is time to go have tea, and talk with the medicine priest or elder about the bear who created a rainbow. The bear is you, he says, and the rainbow is the peace between peoples of different color. This was your vision, but what will you do to make it work in the world?

A Circle of Stones -

TWO WORLDS. Painting by Susan Seddon Boulet.
C The Susan Eleanor Boulet Trust

"ABOUT THE SACRED PIPE"

    The elders say vision seeking megooshaewinun are done also at other times in life, when a person is needing new understanding of their wenjii. Maybe a parent enters the Land of Souls, a lover loves someone else, or someone simply feels "lost" inside. At such a time, a person might find a vision of a Sacred Pipe, or a reason to hold one. This could mean they are ready to accept the care and responsibility for praying with a Sacred Pipe.

    The word for Sacred Pipe used in most areas of Ojibway culture is "Opwaagan" (oh-pwah-gun). The reason it is often called a "peace pipe" is because it was used to make prayers during council meetings to make peace agreements between armies, and because of how Opwaagan was brought to the Anishinaabe people. We will speak more of this in a moment.

It is said by one ancient council of elders, that Sacred Pipes were once held by tribal peoples all around the world. It is said that this gift was taken from the people many thousands of years ago, for reasons that are a mystery. It may have been, that the people were trying to force thigs to happen through the Pipe, or praying only for themselves. The elders say this is not proper use of a Sacred Pipe. So, for many years the people were lost to illness, hunger, and destruction. Finally, the Sacred Pipe was brought back to the people, with new knowledge regarding its proper care, and use in prayer. In Lakota tradition, the Pipe is brought by a goddess, White Buffalo Woman. In Ojibway tradition, it is brought by the great hero of their teaching stories, Nanabush.

Nanabush is both a "symbolic" character, and a real being in the history of Anishinaubek. He stands for the coming of the great star people, and the difficulties they had in learning to have a physical life on the earth. The father of Nanabush is said to be the Keeper of the Land of Souls. His mother is said to be the Morning Star. As his mother dies and returns to the sky when he is born, Nanabush is raised by his grandmother, Old Nokomis. When Nanabush becomes a young man, he thinks his father was the cause of his mother's death, and decides he will fight him. He makes a long journey to the western sky, and finds his father there. They fight one another four days and nights, until finally they agree—neither one can win. But in honor of his strength and bravery, Nanabush is given the sacred "Pipe of Peace" by his father. He is told to take the Pipe to the people, and teach them in

YOUNG MEN SHALL HAVE VISIONS.
Painting by Susan Seddon Boulet.
C The Susan Eleanor Boulet Trust

the ways of proper prayer.

Opwaagan is sacred or "holy" to Native people in a similar way as Jesus is for Christians. A megooshaewin of the Sacred Pipe holds as much spiritual strength for them as a " breaking the bread" ceremony, or "eucharist". Each pinch of tobacco is held up to Kitchi Manido before being placed in the pipe, as prayers are spoken for that pinch. After the fill is complete, puffs are smoked to honor all parts of life. As the smoke rises, it carries the prayers placed into the tobacco up to Kitchi Manido. Styles of filling and smoke varies between communties. (There are many styles of performing megooshaewin with the sacred pipe.)

You may have heard someone speak of drugs being put into a Sacred Pipe. This is not done. It is possible that some young people of other cultures may think it amusing to try this with a pretend pipe they find. But it is not the Native way to do this. Tobaaco, called "semaa" (say-mah) in most Ojibway communities, has for thousands of years been a sacred plant to Native Americans. In traditional Anishinaabe culture, semaa was mixed together with a variety of other plant ingredients to make what is called kiniikinik (kih-nee-kin-nik). This mixture was then used for Sacred Pipe ceremony.

Opwaagan may be found in many forms. There are smaller ones, sometimes made all of stone, which are usually more for personal prayers. Most are in two parts which are joined together for megooshaewin, and separated at closing. In using Opwaagan to pray, each of the four life giving elements is represented, and each of the children of Mother Earth. This creates a balance in the form of Opwaagan which supports all parts of megooshaewin.

The elders have asked that I speak, finally, about the attitude needed to treat Opwaagan as a living being. If one has a vision to hold Opwaagan, one must accept it as one's sacred teacher, and be open to learning. They say Opwaagan will show us deep knowledge about ourselves and life. A Sacred Pipe is not to be used, for example, to ask for power, money, or fame; but instead for the strength and wisdom to do good works for their people. The elders ask that anyone who has had a vision to hold Sacred Pipe please find a pipe teacher, especially a Native elder who is a "pipe carrier", one who is qualified to pray with Opwaagan for the people. This way, it is hoped the true traditions of prayer with Opwaagan can be honored as best as possible.

A Circle of Stones -

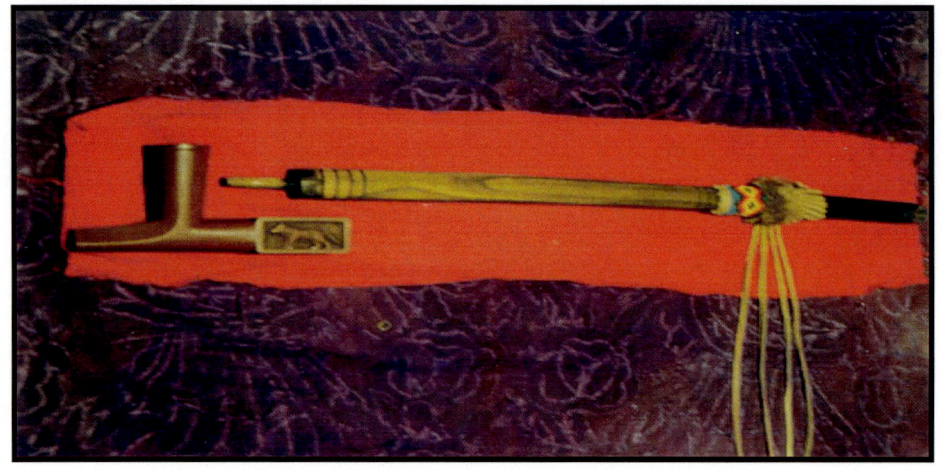

Photo of Opwaagun made by Adam Fortunate Eagle.

SEVENTH STONE
"HOW DID ANISHINAUBEK MAINTAIN GOOD HEALTH?"

We have spoken earlier about how Anishinaabe families liked to bathe often in traditional times; and how it was popular to keep one's home neat and tidy. You also may have learned in other books about how Anishinaabe men hunted and fished; and how the women gathered black rice, grew corn, and made delicious meals. We know now that eating well helps keep people healthy.

We also know now that stress and worry are not good for people's health. I am told by the elders that in traditional times, Anishinaabe people lived in a more relaxed way. There was much hard work to be done, but it was alright to balance this with rest. Events happened when they were ready to happen, like fruit at its time of falling from a branch. No one needed a clock, so people didn't have so much worry or pressure about time. This has been a big difference between Native and European cultures. When Anishinaabeg first started trying to work for American companies, many had trouble accepting rules of keeping to a regular work schedule. Many non-Natives started to think Anishinaabe people were "lazy". This was the beginning of a racist attitude. It has been a spiritual injury for Anishinaabe and other Native people to accept a complete change of life style, especially when it has been forced onto their culture. This kind of injury needs a long time to heal.

"WHAT IS A PURIFICATION LODGE?"

Besides taking care with what comes into one's body, and balancing times of work, rest, and play; it helps people stay healthy to make sure they are removing "toxic" chemicals from their bodies. Some doctors are now saying this is even more important than watching what goes in. "Toxic" chemicals are left over when your body exercises, and digests food. When they don't get released properly, "toxins" can cause illness, aches and pains, and other more serious problems. For many thousands of years, Native people have practiced a way to clear toxins from their bodies. It is called a "purification ceremony". In Northern Ontario, the Ojibway word used is "madootizoon" (muh-do-tih-zone). These ceremonies put together the cleaning of the body, mind, and spirit.

We know it helps the mind relax when it is in a warm, dark, quiet place.

We also know toxins are emitted from our skin when we perspire. We have spoken how the elders say it helps the spirit to have an attitude of prayer. Our spirit contains our hopes and dreams for our lives. It is our creativity and imagination. If all these parts are dull and dreary, we need to have our spirit cleaned.

An Anishinaabe madootizoon takes place in a dome shaped "lodge" covered with furs or blankets. Each sapling used to make the frame is cut with prayers of thanks; and each is placed in a ceremonial way to create what mainstream culture might call a "church". Many stones are placed, with prayers, into a fire which is also made with prayers. People enter the lodge with prayers, and are seated in a ceremonial way inside. The hot stones are then brought, a few at a time, inside and placed in a ceremonial place in the ground. Pinches of cedar and sweetgrass are placed on the stones for blessing. Then, prayer water is sprinkled or poured gently by the leader, onto the stones to make steam. Prayers are spoken or sung by the leader, and by the people in the ceremony.

People in madootizoon ceremony pray for the same kind of things as people do in Christian churches. They pray for themselves, that they may be blessed with good health, strength, courage, generosity, and the will to do good deeds. They pray also for others to be blessed in these ways, and for those who are in hunger, sickness, or other distress to have relief.

A Circle of Stones --------------------------------------

Photo of
Photo of Madootizoon frame.
Courtesy Friends Lake Community.

"IS A MADOOTIZOON LIKE A SAUNA?"

    Steam baths are said to have been used by many cultures around the world. They were reported by the Roman soldiers who traveled to ancient Russia and the British Islands. Saunas and steam rooms are well known in Norway, Denmark, Sweden, and Japan. But historians don't know if prayers were added to make those baths ceremonial. Madootizoon is not a bath. It is not a "sweat lodge". It is a religious ceremony, lead by a highly qualified medicine priest, or elder.

I have been told about, and participated in a variety of madootizoowin, led by Native elders such as Adam Fortunate Eagle, or those qualified by elders. It is not permitted for me to say much about how the ceremonies are done. They are private in a very special way; with each leader having their own style. But it is perhaps good for you to know that purification lodges are done quite often, even in modern times, and for many reasons.

There are "community lodges" for people to maintain general health. Then there are lodge ceremonies held before special occasions such as a wedding, vision seeking ceremony, or a ceremonial dance. Other madootizoowin are done for women at full moon; and still others for healers and those who are in need of healing. One of the most beautiful madootizoowin I have experienced, was done for me after a week of vision seeking in Northern Ontario. The elder who performed the ceremony spent many hours collecting and placing little bits of cedar leaf all around the outside and inside of the lodge. Then she made a tea of cedar and herbs for the water, so the steam had a very fragrant scent.

In modern times, some people in mainstream culture have thought it was "cool" to build a dome of saplings, put some tarps over, throw some hot stones inside, and make up their own idea of a "ceremony". This is of great concern to Native elders. They consider it disrespectful, and that it contributes to the many ways mainstream culture "eats away" the pureness of Native culture.

A Circle of Stones -

"HOW DID ANISHINAUBEK HEAL THOSE WHO WERE ILL OR INJURED?"

When we talk about Anishinaabe medicine and healing, we must remember that in their culture, all forms of life are thought to be made of balanced physical and spiritual parts; and that every event, every movement of life has a true cause, a reason for moving. Modern doctors talk about "symptoms" of a physical problem, and the "cause" of it. The "symptoms" of a cold are having a runny nose and maybe a sore throat. Most people in mainstream culture think the "cause" of a cold is a virus. We might think we caught a cold from someone else, or because our body was too chilled. But we might do well to think about how much stress we place on our immune system, when we consume foods full of antibiotics, preservatives, and hormones; or when we drink alcohol, abuse tobacco, and take synthetic medicines. Then we get closer to the "cause".

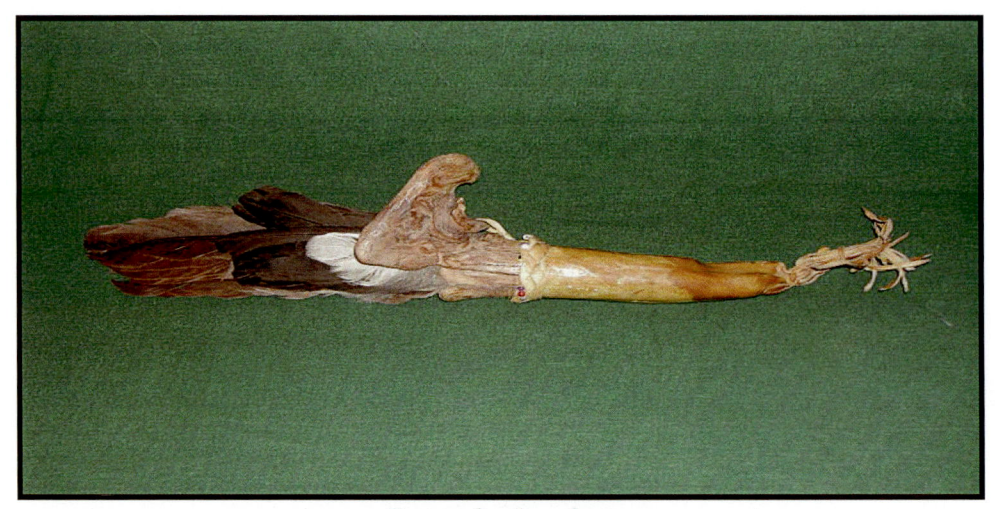

Goose feather fan.
Courtesy Suzanne Eastman.

The elders tell me that in traditional Anishinaabe culture, as well as modern times, there are two parts to healing. The first part is with plant medicines, called "mshkiki" (mesh-kih-kih) by Ojibway in Northern Michigan. Some friends of mine studied the ways of mshkiki for years with an Ojibway elder from Northern Michigan, named Keewadinoquay, which means "Woman of the Northwest Wind". Although Kee's spirit has now traveled to the Land of Souls, her students still meet many times each year to share ideas, and gather plants for mshkiki. I have learned from them that there really are hundreds of plants which can be used in teas, or tinctures and salves to help the symptoms of physical problems.

"WHAT DID A 'MEDICINE MAN' REALLY DO?"

The second part of Native healing methods has been harder for American culture to accept. It is a ceremonial "method" of getting to the cause of a problem, and is often called "shamanic" healing, or "niipakiiwin" (nee-puh-kee-win) in most Ojibway communities. A "method" is a way of doing something, in which one has a special plan with a series of steps to it. Anishinaabe methods are similar in some ways, and different in some ways than other Native methods. But, in the way I have been taught, the methods tend to have a common goal, which is to boost a patient's life force energy. In fact, the goal is to boost life force so much that the patient is able to use their will power to either send away the cause, accept the cause, or both. In this way, niipakiiwin can be successful, even if the patient dies—as long as

A Circle of Stones -

they see the cause, understand it, and come to peace with it.

Some racist attitudes toward Native people were started when movies showed scenes of "medicine men" shaking gourds, chanting, and using drums. First it is good for you to learn that Native healers are often women. The next thing to set strait is the popular mainstream idea that Native people must be "foolish" for thinking their methods would help anyone.

Photo of gourd shaker.
Courtesy Suzanne Downing

Over the years, scientists in the mainstream have become curious about niipakiiwin methods, and set up experiments to see what would happen. They started to notice that some people become ill when exposed to a disease, while others, also exposed, don't become ill. They saw that people more often become ill when they are very sad, or stressed. They found that a steady drumbeat can put a person in a sort of "trance", in which pain can be ignored. As they learned to measure brain waves, the electric energy which carries our thoughts, they discovered that these waves become more balanced and flowing between right and left sides of the brain when a person is hearing or singing Native songs.

I have learned that a gourd, or "shaker" also can be very helpful in changing a person's energy, especially when they are in shock, or "hysterical"—which you might know as "freaked out". The gourd can help them re-orient. A "fan" made with feathers from a bird of prey, such as a hawk, can have the effect of "sweeping" or "pulling" stress and pain out of a patient's body. When I first experienced this, it was truly amazing.

Ancient Native healers didn't have scientific ways to know why their methods worked. They used wisdom instead. Wisdom is what comes from looking at the relatedness of all parts of life. It takes wisdom to look past the symptoms of an illness for the cause. The cause of symptoms of cancer may be the build up of toxins in a person's lymph system. But the "cause of the cause" may be that the person has become disconnected from their meaning and purpose in life. Now niipakiiwin medicine is used by Native healers side by side with mainstream doctors in places like New Mexico, and Michigan, where it is asked for by patients.

"HOW DOES ANISHINAUBEK BECOME TRAINED IN HEALING?"

In Anishinaabe culture, both parts of medicine are handled by members of the Midewewin (mih-day-way-win) Medicine Society. In the Native American world, a "society" is a special organization of which it is not easy to become a member. One must have a vision for this, and go through a difficult "initiation". An "initiation" is like a series of tests. There are purification ceremonies, and special private ceremonies in a Midewewin lodge, under the guidance of the sacred pipe and high level Midewewin leaders. After their initiation, a new member might spent a few years studying the ways of mshkiki before beginning their work with niipakiiwin healing. Then there are many levels or "degrees" of niipakiiwin training, like in Asian martial arts. It truly is as serious, and as deep as medical school training for what is called "western medicine".

The Midewewin Society is many thousands of years old, and still has thousands of members today. New initiations take place each spring, many in Northern Wisconsin.

Seventh Stone

Debwawendunk. Midewewin healer from Bois Fort Reservation.
Courtesy of NAA/Smithsonian Institute.
568A

LAST STONE
"HOW IS ANISHINAABE CULTURE TODAY?"

Today, many Anishinaabe people still live in areas reserved for them by the national governments. They don't have to live there, but many choose this way because they wish to be close to their families, friends, and communities. Many others choose to live more to themselves, but may visit their families and friends at the "reserves", when they are able. There are many of these "reserves" in Michigan, Wisconsin, Minnesota, and throughout Canada.

During the past two hundred years, the national governments of the United States and Canada have tried many ways to solve what they have called the "Indian problem". We have spoken about this in the earlier chapters. At first, in the late 1700's, they set up forts and tried to take over areas by force. Many Eastern Native communities were destroyed or forced to move. But since the communities were spread so far apart, it was difficult for the governments to take control of them all. So the governments decided to make agreements with the tribal councils. They called those agreements "treaties".

Early fort in Northern Michigan.
From original lithograph.

The treaties were written on large pieces of paper, in English, which most council members could not read. In the treaties, the governments offered to buy large amounts of land from the councils. They promised the Anishinaabeg could continue to live as they pleased on the land, traveling wherever they wished to hunt, fish, and trade. But officials presenting the treaties did not mention the small print, which stated the Anishinaabeg would only have this freedom on the land for a few years. After that, they would have to stay in certain areas. Nor did the officials explain about "private property" owned by settlers.

The elders say Anishinaabe hunters often found settlers shooting guns at them, and did not know why.

The land now referred to as "Michigan", was purchased from the Anishinaabe councils in four parts, mostly during the 1800's. The councils were given piles of gold coins, worth a few thousand dollars, and some barrels of whiskey, as their initial payment. The governments promised to pay regular small amounts of money to the councils each year for many years. This money was to be given to Anishinaabe families, but you might guess what happened. The elders say, often the money never was delivered, or never received by the families. They tell of government officials cheating families out of their money, or simply stealing it.

Next, the government of the United States, lead by president Andrew Jackson, in the early 1800's decided to try forcing all Native people living east of the Mississippi River to move west of the river. Soldiers came to get families and make them walk this journey. It was called the "Trail of Tears", and included a few thousand Anishinaabe families, who were brought to a fort at Marshall, Michigan, in ankle chains. Many, many people crossed to the Land of Souls during this journey, especially old ones and children. Many of the families were forced to walk during winter, and to sleep in the open, with no tents. Some were given blankets. But the blankets contained germs of small pox, a deadly illness. It has been said, the soldiers would not let the people stop walking, even to bury those who died.

Then, thieves came to steal possessions from those who slept, and those who had died. The elders tell how those thieves sold many things to museums, which were stolen from people starving and freezing on the Trail of Tears. After two years the program was stopped, and people allowed to return if they could or wished. Those who made it home often found their communities had changed.

"HOW DID THE GOVERNMENTS TRY TO CHANGE ANISHINAUBEK?"

When the "forced move" failed, the governments thought the best plan was to force Native people to give up their culture, and learn to live like everyone in the growing mainstream culture. Part of this plan was to send soldiers to take Native children from their families, and make them live in schools run by Christian churches. The other part was to divide the land into forty acre pieces, and have Native families fill out papers asking to own one of these pieces.

Elders describe many problems with this plan. They say many Native families did not get pieces of land because they couldn't write, or government workers sold pieces to non-Native people who offered them a lot of money. Native families who did get land, could not buy farm machines or seeds because store owners would not sell to Natives. Most of these families found they had to sell their pieces to non-Natives because they could not pay their taxes. It was around this time that the "reserves" were made smaller, and Native religion was put outside the law.

Many Anishinaabe families returned from the "forced move", or from

A Circle of Stones -

trying to become farmers, to live on the "reserves". Some hunting and fishing was still being done, and crafts like baskets being sold, but most families on the "reserves" were caught between the cultures. They were being told they couldn't live in the old way, but had no money to live in the "new way". Many of the men tried working for tree cutting companies, paper mills, and steel mills, but it was hard for them to be away from their culture, and their communities. Many turned to drinking to dull the pain of their incredible loss and emptiness. Since the Christian boarding schools used assault and battery as a way of punishment, a few generations of Anishinaabe children grew up with deep shame and rage, which they then took out on each other, and their families.

Ojibway family, early 1900's.
Courtesy Minnesota Historical Society.

Elders tell of this shame and rage being passed down through families even today.

By the later 1800's, most, if not all of the treaties made between the governments and the Anishinaabeg had been broken by the governments. The American government was working on downsizing reserves all over the country, and forging laws forbidding Native people from practicing their religion, speaking their language, singing their songs, dancing their dances, or meeting in tribal council. The Bureau of Indian Affairs, or BIA, was created by the government to take over managing life on the

Young Anishinaabe women, early 1900's.
Courtesy Bentley Historical Library.

reserves. BIA officials were supposed to take the role of "governing" on the reserves, replacing the "tribal councils". The BIA created police departments, courts, and jails on the reserves. They were then supposed to make sure no one was practicing traditional culture.

By the 1920's, Anishinaabeg living either on the reserves, or in cities, were suffering terribly. As agencies like Catholic Social Services, and Michigan State Social Services were formed, they sent "welfare workers" to "rescue" Anishinaabe infants and children, whose parents were having too many problems, or were too poor, to "properly" care for them. The elders state bitterly, that in countless cases, decisions were made by white welfare workers to place Anishinaabe infants and children into white foster families, rather than find relatives to provide care. Once in the foster homes, elders say, the children were usually not allowed contact with their original family members. Richard Wagamese, an Ojibway man from Canada, tells of his experience with foster care, and how he finally was found by his original family, in his book <u>Keeper 'N Me.</u>

Another program, started in the mid 1900's, was the Indian Relocation plan. The American government has used the BIA to encourage Native families to move from the reserves to a number of American cities. The idea was, that the BIA would then help the families with housing, training, and employment. But many have reported being placed in "ghetto" housing, and being set up with low paying, "dead-end" jobs. Then, they are basically "trapped" in the cities, with no means to return to the reserves. One of the boys with whom I worked in Michigan's schools, told how his mother, a full-blood Arapaho, had been placed in foster care after her family had relocated to Chicago. Many elders believe this is yet another tactic of the government, to separate the families, thereby weakening the bonds of community which hold together Native culture.

"HOW HAS ANISHINAUBEK TRIED TO FIT WITH MAINSTREAM CULTURE?"

In the 1900's Native people slowly started to get back some rights to practice their religion, language, culture, and small portions of their land. Often this has been accomplished through the legal system. They also gained the right to vote. Many fought as soldiers for the governments in the World Wars, Korean, and Vietnam Wars. Thousands have been through college and become teachers, doctors, lawyers, and engineers; while others have become respected as strong and skilled workers in mills, factories and construction. Some have won medals at the Olympics, and others have been elected to be part of the congress or parliament.

Today, many Native leaders in America and Canada have urged their tribes to establish themselves as "nations", independent from American or Canadian governments. In the 1960's and 70's, the American Indian Movement, AIM, with many courageous leaders, including Dennis Banks, and Clyde Bellecourt, both Ojibway, protested racist government policies, and fought for the right of Indian nations to govern themselves. They also have tried to expose racist practices in mainstream culture, which depict Native people as ignorant or foolish.

Anishinaabe tribes and bands have put energy and money into building "casinos" on their land, where people can come to try winning money by betting. A lot of money has been coming back to Anishinaabe communities from these projects. Some elders think casinos are not good, and that money earned from them is not being spent wisely. But in Anishinaabe communities, much of the money has been used to build or operate special schools and cultural centers like the Gchii Mukwa (Big Bear) Recreation Center in Sault St. Marie, Michigan, or the seventh Generation Program in Mt. Pleasant, Michigan, where traditional values and history can be taught, and community gatherings held. At Gchii Mukwa there is also space for hockey and basketball.

Many Anishishaabe families have turned to Christianity. Others live either by traditional ways, or belong to the Native American Church, which blends traditional and Christian beliefs.

"WHAT IS A "POW-WOW?"

A "Pow-Wow" is partly a ceremonial dance, and partly a dance competition. Native dancers come from many parts of the United States and Canada to dance in celebration of their heritage. There also are Native "drum teams" which drum and sing for the dances; and Native artists and traders who sell their art, jewelry, blankets, animal furs, and many other items. At most Pow-Wow's Native foods, like stew made with corn and buffalo or elk meat, are served. Many times all the members of a family may join in dancing, even younger children.

Some of the dances at a Pow-Wow are called "Inter-tribal Dances". Those dances last for the length of one song, and include anyone who wishes to join. Everyone steps in their own style, and moves slowly clockwise in a circle around the arena. This circle represents the Circle of Life, in the way we spoke earlier. Since the Circle of Life includes all races and cultures, everyone is welcome to dance at those times. To dance in the Great Circle is to celebrate the beauty of one's true self, and one's connection to all people and parts of nature.

Honoring Dances are also done to honor "veterans", those who have served in the military for their country. Others are done to honor a birthday, or wedding, or their first time dancing. Sometimes there may be a "couples" dance, in which couples who are married, or sweethearts can dance the Great Circle together holding hands. In this kind, young "maidens" who don't yet have a sweetheart can go to the guys on the side, and ask one to dance just for fun. If you're a guy, you can imagine being very happy to be chosen, or very unhappy!

Another kind of dancing at Pow-Wow's is done to win prizes. There are many "categories", or ways to enter contest dancing. Some are for age levels, and some are for style of dance. In men's "traditional style" dancing, the costumes use hunting bird feathers in natural color. Those dance steps follow a more focused pattern, in which the dancer is hunting for the strongest meaning of their life. Men's contest dancing includes other styles, like "grass dance" and "fancy dance". Grass dancers have long fringes on their costumes and move like prairie grass flowing in a breeze. Fancy dancers use bright colored feathers formed into large circles for their costumes; and whirl around from side to side.

Women's dance styles include "Women's Traditional" and "Fancy Shawl", in which they are expressing the honor of their life, and another style called "Jingle Dress". There are a few versions of the story hof how "Jingle Dress" came to the People. As it was told to me, this dance came from a vision found by a woman many years ago. It was a vision about

A Circle of Stones -

healing for the world, and showed the woman a picture of the jingle dress, with little metal cones sewn onto it. Because of this, those who wish to dance this dance must join the Jingle Dress Society, and keep some promises about helping the world to heal. This dance is popular with teens as well as adults.

Photo of Pow-Wow Intertribal.
Courtesy Faye Costello

Anishinaabe culture is growing, giving new life to traditional values, ways of life, language, and prayer. But it also is trading parts of itself with parts of mainstream culture. You may notice how many people have "dream catchers" hanging in their front car window. This is a part of Anishinaabe culture which has become very popular. If you visit an Anishinaabe community, the parents of teenagers may tell you how their children want to wear designer jeans, rent video games, and eat at McDonalds. The Anishinaabe teens I have met tell me they don't want to be on display, or talk much about traditional culture. They want to be free to live how they wish, think how they wish, and to be respected both for who they are as a Native American, and as a member of the mainstream like everyone else.

I hope, by reading this book, you have come to have more understanding of Anishinaabe culture, and its people. Perhaps you will let others know what you have learned; or perhaps you will decide to look for a Native elder, from whom you may learn more. Perhaps you will become a healer, helping to make life better for others. Or, perhaps you will become a lawyer, and help the Anishinaabeg protect their sovereignty as a nation, and the integrity of their culture. Whatever it is you become, I wish you well on your life's journey. Apaegish mino-kummee-in ae-ani-izauyin.

BIBLIOGRAPHY

Benton-Benai, Edward. <u>The Mishomis Book. The Voice of the Ojibway</u>. St. Paul, MN: Indian Country Press, Inc. 1979.

Blackbird, Andrew J. (Chief Mack-e-te-be-nessy). <u>History of the Ottawa and Chippewa Indians of Michigan</u>. Ypsilanti, MI: Job Printing House, 1887.

Blessing, Fred K. <u>The Ojibway Indians Observed</u>. St. Paul, MN: Minnesota Archeological Society, 1977.

Clifton, James A., Cornell, George L., McClurken, James M. <u>People of The Three Fires</u>. Grand Rapids, MI: Michigan Indian Press. Grand Rapids Inter-tribal Council, 1986.

Danzinger, Edmund Jefferson Jr. <u>The Chippewas of Lake Superior</u>. Norman, OK: University of Oklahoma Press, 1979.

Deloria, Vine Jr., Lytle, Clifford. <u>The Nations Within: The Past and Future of American Indian Sovereignty</u>. New York, NY: Random House, Inc., 1984.

Densmore, Frances. <u>Chippewa Music</u>. Volumes I and II. City: Ross & Haines, Inc., 1973 (re-issue).

Densmore, Frances. <u>Chippewa Customs</u>. St. Paul, MN: Minnesota Historical Society Press, 1979

Deur, Lynne. <u>Nishnawbe. A Story of Indians in Michigan</u>. City: River Road Publications, 1981

Dewdney, Selwyn. <u>Sacred Scrolls of the Southern Ojibway</u>. Toronto: University of Toronto Press, 1975

Eklund, Coy. <u>A Chippewa Language Workbook</u>. Ann Arbor, MI: Ann Arbor Public Library.

Frazier, Jean. <u>Kah-Wam-Da-Meh. A Study of Michigan's Major Indian Tribes</u>. City: Herman E. Cameron Memorial Foundation, Inc., 1988

Johnston, Basil. <u>Ojibway Ceremonies</u>. City: McClelland & Stuart, 1982; Lincoln, NE: University of Nebraska Press, 1990.

Johnston, Basil. <u>Ojibway Heritage</u>. City: McClelland & Stuart 1976; Lincoln, NE: University of Nebraska Press, 1990.

Keewaydinoquay. <u>Puhpohwee for the People. A Narrative Account of Some Uses of Fungi aong the Anishinaabe</u>. Cambridge, MA: Botanical Museum of Harvard University, 1978.

Knietz, Vernon W. Indians of the Western Great Lakes. Ann Arbor, MI: University of Michigan Press, 1940.

Lyford, Carrie A. Ojibwa Crafts. City: R. Schneider, Publishers, 1982.

Morey, Sylvester: Gillian, Olivia L. Respect for Life. Traditional Upbringing of American Indian Children. City: The Myrin Institute, Inc., 1974.

Quimby, George I. Indian Life in the Upper Great Lakes. Chicago: University of Chicago Press, 1960.

Rhodes, Richard A. Eastern Ojibwa-Chippewa-Ottawa Dictionary. Berlin-New York: Mouton de Gruyter, 1993.

Smart, Alton Sonny. Nind inawmaagan Bimaadizi Wawii ye bii'ige. (The Life of My Relatives). Lac Du Flambeau, WI: Parenting Program Curriculum, Lac Du Flameau Family Resource Center, 1987.

Vizenor, Carl. The People Named Chippewa: Narrative Histories. St. Paul: University of Minnesota Press, 1984.

Tanner, Helen Hornbeck. Indians of North America: The Ojibwa. New York, Philadelphia: Newberry Library, Chelsea House Publishers, 1992.

Bibliography

Waldman, Carl. <u>Atlas of the North American Indian</u>. New York: Facts of File Publications, 1985.